LEARN TANTRIC SEX

USING TANTRA TO INCREASE SEXUAL PLEASURE

AVENTURAS DE VIAJE

Illustrated by
SHUMONA MALLICK

Copyright SF Nonfiction Books © 2014

www.SFNonfictionBooks.com

All Rights Reserved

No part of this document may be reproduced without written consent from the author.

WARNINGS AND DISCLAIMERS

The information in this publication is made public for reference only.

Neither the author, publisher, nor anyone else involved in the production of this publication is responsible for how the reader uses the information or the result of his/her actions.

CONTENTS

Understanding Tantric Sex	1
The Mindset of an Amazing Sexual Being	4
Your Tantric Space	5
Chakras	6
Namaste Ritual	7
Tantric Taste Test	8
Breathing	10
Understanding and Improving Orgasm	14
Self-Exploration	19
Masturbation	23
Redirecting Sexual Energy	29
Peaking	31
Tantric Massage	33
Tantric Dancing	35
Tantric Oral	38
Sexual Poses for Tantric Sex	39
After Climax	41
30 More Tantric Meditations and Exercises	42
References	55
Author Recommendations	57
About Aventuras	59

THANKS FOR YOUR PURCHASE

Did you know you can get FREE chapters of any SF Nonfiction Book you want?

https://offers.SFNonfictionBooks.com/Free-Chapters

You will also be among the first to know of FREE review copies, discount offers, bonus content, and more.

Go to:

https://offers.SFNonfictionBooks.com/Free-Chapters

Thanks again for your support.

UNDERSTANDING TANTRIC SEX

Tantra is a spiritual practice in which connection and the full experience of sex is valued over orgasm. Practitioners combine sexual energy to enhance the connection between them and the universe. With tantric sex, you can expect longer sexual interaction and whole-body experiences.

When practicing tantra, do it in a space conducive to meditation (see Your Tantric Space). Stay present and pay attention to the feelings in your body, your breathing, and the movement of your and your lover's energy rising up through the body and into the universe.

Build sexual excitement, and then move the sexual energy around. Don't get lost in the moment as you would during normal intercourse. When you climax, if you are in full awareness of the state and stay there for as long as possible, you can bring yourself to a state of enlightenment.

Tantra is meant to be fun and playful. Some concepts and meditations may be a bit too much for some, but lower your inhibitions and you will discover sexual bliss and a focused spirit. Allow the pleasure to come to you, as opposed to striving for it.

Although the focus of this book is on tantric sex, there are a few non-tantric sex exercises. This is because you first need to be in tune with yourself and your partner as sexual beings on a basic level before moving on to tantric sex.

It is, of course, highly possible that since you are reading a book about tantric sex that you are already in tune with your sexual being. Just do whatever you wish to do.

At first, you may feel some of these meditations are too "out there." Experiment with what you are comfortable with. After a time, you may wish to try others. Do what you want, when you want, for however long you want, and have fun doing it.

Some of these meditations can only be done with a partner (preferably a lover), but many of them can be adapted to solo meditation.

If you do not have a current lover, or your lover is not open to tantra, try searching online for tantra partners.

Creating a Deeper Connection

When you practice tantra, you will connect with the universe in a way most people never imagine. When you practice tantra with your lover, the connection between you will become deeper than ever. When you practice tantra through sex, you will experience the deepest possible physical pleasure.

Some ways to make this connection are:

- Listening to each other with unconditional acceptance and without trying to solve the problem.
- Showing daily physical affection without the expectation of sex.
- Making love with full consciousness.
- Practicing partnered yoga.
- Practicing the many tantric exercises outlined in this publication together.

Being the Witness

While practicing tantra, whether meditative or during sex, observe what you are doing while you are doing it. If you get distracted or anxious, notice these thoughts, then refocus on your breath and the physical sensations in your body.

Related Chapters:

- Your Tantric Space
- Breathing

THE MINDSET OF AN AMAZING SEXUAL BEING

Believe you are an erotic sexual being.

Sex is pleasure. It heals and is healthy.

Have an open mind and be open to your lover.

Release your inhibitions and discover what truly makes you feel good.

Devote your whole self, mind and body, to the moment. Give your all to your lover and receive all that you can.

Feel your whole body, as opposed to just focusing on orgasm.

There's nothing wrong with having a lot of sex. The only way you can have too much sex is if it affects your life in a negative way, such that you neglect work or family, for example.

YOUR TANTRIC SPACE

You will get the most out of your tantric practices if you have a special space that can accumulate the energy.

This space need not be exclusively for tantric practice, but it should be conducive to the practice. Most, if not all, of your tantric practices should be performed in this space.

Fortunately, a tantric space is very conducive to other activities of a similar spiritual/healing/calming nature, such as massage, meditation, yoga, or sleeping. Many people use their bedroom.

The basic principle is to create the right mood by stimulating the senses, and to have everything you will need within easy reach so as to not disturb the mood.

Here are some examples:

- Make a tidy area with soft pillows and comfortable bed sheets (silk, velvet, satin, cotton, etc.).
- Have fresh flowers and incense (jasmine or musk).
- Light candles and/or use dimmed lights.
- Put on some tranquil or sensual music.
- Have mirrors, toys, feathers, silk scarves, and massage oil nearby.
- Have things to pleasure the taste buds, such as honey, chocolate, or grapes.

CHAKRAS

Chakras are the energy centers in your body. Ideally, energy flows freely through them and in a balanced manner. When energy is not flowing freely, it leads to illness, emotional upset, etc.

The chakras are often referred to in tantric sex or yoga.

From bottom to top are the names of the chakras and where they are located.

1st : Root/Base : Base of the spine.

2nd: Sacral : Lower abdomen.

3rd : Solar Plexus : Upper abdomen.

4th : Heart : Just above the heart.

5th : Throat : Throat

6th : Third Eye : Forehead between the eyes.

7th : Crown : Very top of the head.

NAMASTE RITUAL

The Namaste ritual is a beautiful gesture of respect and love between you, your tantric partner, and the universe. Use it to begin and/or end your tantric meditations. Kneel opposite one another.

Rest your buttocks on your heels and put your hands together in the praying position.

Gaze into each other's eyes. If it is the beginning of the meditation, raise your hands into the sky and bow to honor each other.

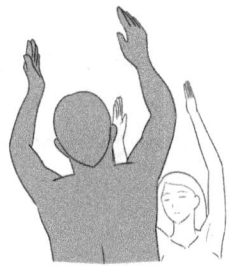

If you are closing the meditation with it, there is no need to raise your hands.

After the bow, bring your hands back into the prayer position, gaze into each other's eyes and say "Namaste" (na-mas-tay).

TANTRIC TASTE TEST

Sit naked across from your lover. Look deeply into their eyes, into their soul. Describe to each other how much you love and respect one another, and how you wish to become together in the universe.

Take each other's hands and close your eyes. Breathe deeply and in sync, inhaling and exhaling at the same time. Feel the energy flowing within yourselves and between your bodies, especially at your chakras. Without touching each other, glide your hands around each other's bodies. Feel the warm energy radiating from each other.

Open your eyes and join hands again. Gaze into each other's souls. Continue to breathe in sync. Concentrate on the energy flowing between you through your hands, breathing, and eyes.

When you're ready, slowly and softly touch each other's genitals. Once you are very wet and your partner is hard, or begin to make love. When you are ready, or during sex, engage in the Yab Yum position.

Yab Yum

The Yab Yum position can be used to rest and/or embrace each other in a sexual or non-sexual way. It is a very intimate position, and is also good for being still and delaying orgasm. The man sits cross-legged, and the woman sits on top of him, wrapping her legs behind his back.

Related Chapters:

- Chakras

BREATHING

Proper breathing plays a big part in connecting with yourself, your lover, and the universe. It is life force.

Full-Stomach Breathing

With your mouth closed, breathe in deeply through your nose. Count to four as you do so.

Your ribs and stomach expand as you fill up with air.

As you inhale, imagine your body and chakras being filled with the clear, positive energies of love and happiness.

When you cannot breathe in any more, hold the breath for a count of two, then fully exhale to a count of four through your nose and/or mouth, pushing your stomach to your spine.

Imagine all cloudy toxins, stress and negativity exiting your body.

Synchronized Breathing

Breathe in and out at the same time as your partner. This can be done at any time in any position, but is particularly good for sharing energy when spooning.

Circular Breathing

Sit opposite your partner and breathe deeply in sync, so that you are breathing in while they are breathing out.

As you breathe out and they breathe in, imagine the energy exiting your heart and entering theirs. As they breathe out and you breathe in, imagine the energy flowing out into the ground and back up into you. After a few minutes, swap it around.

This can also be done during sex.

Firing up Sexual Energy

As you inhale, use your hand to trace where it stops.

Lower your hand so each breath comes from your genitals.

Sitting Expansion

From a comfortable sitting position, compact yourself as much as possible.

Bring your elbows in and rest your hands on your head. Your spine will stretch.

As you inhale, expand your body.

Keep your hands where they are, but stretch your elbows as far back as you can and arch your back. Your chest will stretch.

Repeat.

Balloons

Allow your arms to dangle comfortably by your sides.

Exhale forcefully until your lungs are completely empty. Allow yourself to make noise.

Inhale just as forcefully, with as much or more sound. Continue this, being more forceful and louder with each breath.

Energizing Rapid Breath

With your arms outstretched to your sides, breathe rapidly through your nose. Pump your arms up and down. Your stomach should pulsate quickly.

Energizing Your Chakras

Sit back-to-back with your lover.

Direct your breath into your first chakra. Don't try to control it. Allow it to be chaotic and allow your body to move in the same fashion.

When you are ready, direct your breath into your second chakra in the same manner. Also allow your body to move. Continue in this way through all your chakras.

Once you reach the crown, work your way back down, allowing your breath to calm down. Once you are at your first chakra again, just feel your chakras vibrating in unison.

Note: Changing your position—sitting face to face or lying next to each other, for example—will change the sensations.

Lama Breaths

Stand with your feet shoulder-width apart and your knees slightly bent.

As you inhale, raise your arms to out to your sides. On the exhale, drop your arms to the side of your body. Allow sound to be expelled as you breathe out. Repeat this.

When you're ready, inhale and only raise one arm until you have a fist above your head. Drop it on the exhale, allowing sound to come out.

Alternate arms and repeat.

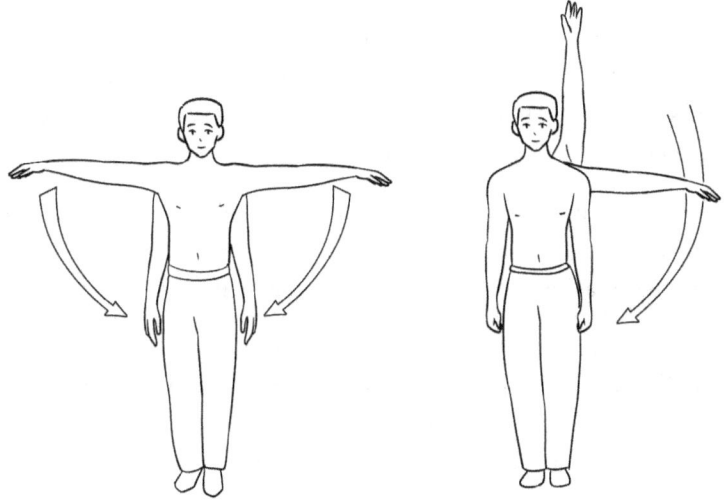

Related Chapters:

- Chakras

UNDERSTANDING AND IMPROVING ORGASM

One of the keys to having amazing sex is to not focus on orgasm. In fact, focusing on orgasm often inhibits having amazing orgasms.

Instead, enjoy your body for everything it is. Then when you do climax, it will feel incredible.

Note: Orgasms may release unexpected emotions. All reactions are healthy.

Her Orgasm

Women need mental focus much more and then men do to reach climax, and many women have never experienced orgasm. This may be due to low testosterone levels, but a more likely reason is psychological barriers.

Note: If it is due to low testosterone levels try switching to barrier methods of birth control (e.g., condoms) as other methods may be upsetting your hormonal balance.

The first step to overcoming psychological barriers is to feel good about orgasms and enjoy sex. It isn't a bad thing, it's amazing. If the barriers are deeply rooted—in sexual abuse, for instance—then a therapist may be helpful.

Going solo (masturbation) is the most reliable way for most women to experience their first orgasm. Go somewhere where you feel relaxed and won't be disturbed, and where you can express yourself freely. Don't try to control your body or worry about what it is doing. Just let it happen. Once you can give yourself an orgasm, it will be easier to have one with your lover.

Many women need more than just penetration to climax. Stimulate the clitoris at the same time.

Women: Never fake orgasms! It will only teach your lover how not to satisfy you.

Men: The only real way you can tell if a woman is having an orgasm is if you feel the intense contractions deep inside her vagina.

Simultaneous Orgasm

In order to climax together, you need to reach the same level of arousal at the same time.

More often than not, it is the man who is ready to climax first. He can delay penetration until she is close, then with communication they can climax together.

Something to think about: If you climax together, you may be too focused on your own orgasm to fully experience the climax of your lover.

Multiple Orgasms

The key is to build up a greater level of sexual tension. Spend more time working each other up.

Men and women can have multiple orgasms. The only difference is that men will have a physical downtime that women will not.

Men can achieve multiple orgasms without the downtime by strengthening their PC muscles. When you are close to ejaculation, tense your PC muscle to restrict the release of fluid while still feeling the contractions of the orgasm.

Note: Some consider this practice unnatural and dangerous.

After your first orgasm, the clitoris or penis may be too sensitive for more direct stimulation. Back off a bit. Shorten your down time by taking deep breaths and rocking your pelvis in time to your breathing.

Intensifying Orgasm

Stimulate erogenous zones during the orgasm and allow yourself to fully let go, making spontaneous and uncensored sounds and movement.

If you have the fortitude, you can intensify your orgasm by foregoing it every two out of three times. Doing so increases desire and will intensify emotional and physical response in those times when you do allow yourself to orgasm.

Intensifying orgasm can also be achieved by strengthening your sexual muscles. Distinguishing between the two different muscles will become clearer as you strengthen them. Do these two exercises once a day, every day. Do 10-50 repetitions.

1. Sit or stand comfortably. As you breathe in, squeeze your anus, keeping the rest of your genital area relaxed. Breathe out and relax.
2. Breathe in deeply and hold your breath. Squeeze your genitals, making sure that the muscles in your anus are relaxed. Breathe out and relax.

PC (Pubococcygeal) Muscle

Strengthening the PC muscle is beneficial for everyone. Women can make their vaginas tighter and may also have stronger orgasms. Men have reported stronger erections and greater control of ejaculation. When you start and stop the flow of your urine, you are engaging your PC muscle.

Ways Women Can Exercise Their PC Muscle

- Tighten and relax the PC muscle 10 times in a row (10 reps). Do 10 sets of these, making a total of 100 reps. Do this twice a day, for 200 reps per day.
- Tighten and hold for three to seven seconds, and then release. Do 10 reps twice a day.
- Slowly tighten the PC muscle, stopping every now and again on the way up. Do 10 reps twice a day.
- When the PC muscle is strong enough, a woman can flex it during sex to grip her lover's penis. She may even be able to bring him to climax just by doing this.

Ways Men Can Exercise Their PC muscle

- Flex it 10 times in a row, for 10 sets per session, twice a day.
- A man can do it during intercourse to have his penis move inside his lover.

Tantric PC Exercise

Use your PC muscle to send your sexual energy through your body. As you engage the muscle, inhale through your nose. Hold your breath while you release and tense the muscle as many times as you can before you release your breath back out through your nose.

Tantric Orgasm

As you climax, tune into your body and surroundings, as opposed to blocking the world out by shutting your eyes. By doing so, you can achieve a state of bliss and your whole body will vibrate in orgasm.

As you approach climax, relax and let your body ease into it. Take deep, conscious breaths and focus on the feelings in every part of your body. As you climax, keep your eyes open and gaze into your lover's eyes.

Note: Although not necessary to achieve tantric orgasm, being in love will further enhance the experience.

After some practice, you can learn to store the sexual energy you and your lover create during sex in any part of your body, and then access it at will. You can also send the energy out into the universe through your crown chakra.

Related Chapters:

- Breathing
- Masturbation

SELF-EXPLORATION

Explore your body. Learn what feels good to you. Start by giving yourself a full-bodied massage from head to toes. Take your time touching every part of your body. Use different pressures and strokes. Take deep breaths.

Erogenous Zones

Erogenous zones are the parts of the body that respond to sexual stimulation. Any part of the body may arouse a person, depending on the individual. Test by stroking, licking, sucking, kissing, caressing and gently biting any and all parts of your lover's body, taking note of what they respond to favorably.

Her Pleasure Points (Vagina)

Clitoris: As far as we know, the only purpose of the clitoris is to give women pleasure! It is located at the top of the labia, above the vagina, and is covered by the clitoral hood, which protects it from being constantly stimulated. This small bud-like erogenous zone swells with excitement, but once it is very aroused it may appear to disappear. Gentle rubbing usually feels fantastic to the owner.

G-spot: This area is about one third of the way up on the front wall of the vagina, and feels like a small swelling. When it is stimulated many women feel intense pleasure and some may even "ejaculate." Others may feel discomfort or numbness. Stimulate the G-spot by rubbing the making a "come here" motion with the pad of your finger, or use a vibrator with a special G-spot attachment.

Note: For double the pleasure, stimulate the clitoris and G-spot at the same time.

Perineum: The area of skin between the vagina and the anus. Use gentle strokes with your fingers or tongue.

His Pleasure Points (Penis)

Frenulum: The tiny bump of skin near the indentation on the underside of the penis.

Coronal ridge: The ring-like ridge around the head of the penis. Lick underneath it.

Perineum: The area of skin between the base of the penis and the anus. Use gentle strokes with your fingers or tongue.

Prostate gland: A small gland that lies below the bladder and can be stimulated via anal penetration. "Prostate" is not the same as prostrate.

Head: The smooth head of the penis.

Shaft: The area spanning from the base to the coronal ridge.

Scrotum: The sack that hangs below the penis and contains the testes.

Tantric Self-Exploration

Although these exercises are for self-exploration, they can also be done with a lover.

Emotional Release

Place something soft, which you can safely hit in front of you, such as some pillows. Have something from nature, like a leaf, next to you as well.

Put on some loud music; kneel before the pillows and release your anger into them. Bury your head in them, shout at them, and hit them. Become angry and use all the emotion you can. Shout anything you want.

Note: If you are doing this with your lover, you should not be able to hear each other's words.

When you feel like it, sit quietly. Express whatever emotions surface.

When everything is released and you are still, take your natural object and imagine all the clutter in your mind flowing into it, then return it to nature or give it to your lover to do so.

Friends with Nature

Go somewhere with nature around, such as a forest or a park. Walk around until a leaf (or flower, tree, etc.) "calls" you. Take the leaf and study it. Really feel it and see deep into it. Feel its life force.

Thought-Writing

Take a pen and paper and begin to write uncensored. Just write continuously, even if it doesn't make sense.

After five minutes, read the words out loud to yourself, being aware of how you are responding to what you read.

When you're ready, throw the paper away, along with all the clutter of your mind. Burn it if you wish.

Releasing Orgasmic Potential

Put on some loud, energetic music and get comfortable.

Begin to move your pelvis. Touch your genitals slowly and sensually. Massage your stomach, allowing your sexual energy to flow into it. Make any sounds you wish.

Continue to move however you feel, letting your hands roam anywhere on your body. Allow the energy to rise up through your solar plexus into and your heart. Allow the pressure to build until the energy finally bursts through.

Release any emotions as they come and surrender to the universe.

MASTURBATION

Just like sex, masturbation is only unhealthy if it interferes negatively with your life or if it causes severe physical pain or damage. It is the best way to discover what you enjoy sexually.

Use what you learn from masturbation to enhance your sex life by talking about it with your lover. Masturbating in front of each other is another great way to learn. It is also highly erotic.

Start with scented candles and a long bath. After the bath, give yourself a full body massage whilst concentrating on your breathing.

Finally, stimulate yourself sexually. Don't think about the orgasm. Just enjoy the touch.

When you're ready, bring yourself to climax.

Mutual Masturbation

When you're getting your lover off, enjoy it. If it turns you on, then they will get even more turned on. You can masturbate yourself at the same time, or they can give you a hand.

Once you find a stroke they like focus on the rhythm and pressure, and don't forget about the rest of their body. Their genitalia may become very sensitive immediately after climax, so ease off.

Tease

Caress the area around your partner's genitals sensually, without directly stimulating them. Come close then move away again.

Get closer and closer and then gradually skim the erogenous zone. Take your time, until your partner is very aroused.

Only then should you move in for masturbation, but continue to move away every now and again. Two steps forward and one step back.

When your partner is on the verge of orgasm, keep a steady pace and keep doing what they like most. After they climax, ease off, unless told not to.

For Him

- Use a back-and-forth motion from the base to the head.
- Concentrate on the head of the penis. Use one hand just on the head, and one going up and down the shaft.
- Use one hand to press down on the base of the penis, while the other goes up and down the shaft.
- Play with the scrotum and testicles at the same time as the penis.
- Holding the penis with your left hand, place your right palm across the head. After every up-and-down with your left hand, rub your right hand lightly in a circle on the head.
- Have both hands on the penis, one at the top and one at the bottom. As your top hand comes down, bring your bottom hand up. Your hands should meet in the middle. Then, as your bottom hand goes back down, bring your top hand back up. Repeat.
- Use the same technique as above, but twist each hand a little as you do it.
- Use your thumb and forefinger to form a ring around the penis. Do it with both hands. Run your fingers

up and down the penis any way you want: up and down together, with a twist, in opposite directions, etc.
- Coat your hands with a mild skin scrub. Gently roll the penis back and forward between your hands.
- Wrap a thin or silky scarf around the penis and use a gentle stroke, twisting occasionally. Move the skin under the scarf or move the scarf itself.
- Fill a condom with as much jelly as it will hold (warm or cold) then put it on the penis. Expect jelly to displace. Once it has settled, hold the condom tight at the opening to seal the remaining jelly in. Use your other hand on the shaft.
- Grip the top of the penis with your left hand and place the right hand underneath the testicles, with your fingers pointing toward the anus. As you slide your left hand down, bring your right hand up, so they meet near the base of the penis. From here, slide your left hand back up the penis and your right hand back down, toward the anus.
- When ejaculation begins, clasp your two hands around the head of the penis. Squeeze gently and release in time with the contractions.
- Lightly brush your fingers up the shaft and around the tip.
- Work your hand up and down, tightening and releasing your grip as you go.
- Put the penis between your two open hands. Roll it in your palms as you move up and down.
- Gently toss the penis from one hand to another.
- Firmly hold the base with one hand. With your other hand, alternate between making circles at the tip and pulling the head up while gently twisting it.

- With your hands, squeeze the muscles that connect the thigh with the genital area.

For Her

- Lubrication, either natural or store-bought, is great for everyone, but a woman needs it to get a pleasurable experience more than a man does.
- Stimulate the clitoris by rubbing it directly or with a pillow, water flow from the shower, dildo, etc.
- Rub on or pull at the skin above and around the clitoris.
- Penetrate the vagina with your fingers or an object while also providing clitoral stimulation.
- When climaxing, place your hand over the pubic mound, with your fingers curved inside the front of the vagina, and pull up with slight pressure. You can pulse your fingers in time with the contractions.
- Many women report that the area to the left of their clitoris (as they look down), when rubbed, gives the most pleasure.
- Pull back the clitoral hood with one hand and stimulate the tip of the clitoris.
- Use a short up-and-down stroke on one side of the clitoris.
- Twirl your finger on the clitoral head, then around it. Move in both directions.
- Stimulate the lower part of the vaginal entrance, where it meets with the perineum.
- Push down on the G-spot with the pads of your finger(s) with varying pressures.
- Use your thumbs to twirl around the nipples, then at the far side of each breast.

- Stroke the perineum with two fingers while using your thumb on the clitoris.
- Rub the clitoral tip in circles, using a feather-light touch.
- If direct clitoral stimulation is too intense, rub on top of the clitoral hood.
- Rub around the vagina and labia.
- Rub up and down the opening between the labia, on the labia, and around the vagina.
- Stimulate the clitoris and the G-spot at the same time.

Tantric Hand Job

As you pleasure your lover in this way, compliment them throughout the whole process.

Your lover lies comfortably on their back. Run your hands smoothly over their body, and then let them rest, one at the top of the spine and one at the base of the spine. If either of these spots is cold, warm it up with your love energy.

Oil your lover's skin liberally and use your whole body to rub them all over. Rub their back and legs, then turn them over and rub their chest. Gaze into your lover's eyes and encourage sounds of pleasure.

Run your hands from the groin to the heart to transfer sexual energy into love. Send your love through your hands as well.

After you have massaged your lover's entire body, concentrate on their groin. If they are going to climax, just ease off for a while until their excitement subsides. You can continue to move energy from the groin to the heart.

Reassure them that climax or even arousal (including erections or wetness) is not important. Just feeling the pleasure of touch is amazing, and if arousal or climax happens then that is also fine.

Continue to rub the groin using any strokes you wish. Vary your touches and stay tuned into your lover's energy.

Related Chapters:

- Breathing

REDIRECTING SEXUAL ENERGY

When we are aroused, we build up a lot of energy. We can either release this energy or carry it round with us. We usually release it through climax. When you do not release it, you will experience what some may refer to as "sexual frustration," but in fact, if utilized in the right way, this energy can help people become very productive in their everyday lives.

We can make the most of this sexual energy by redirecting it throughout the body. By doing so, instead of feeling frustration when we are aroused but unable to release, we will feel energized throughout the body.

This redirection is also the first step in experiencing a full body orgasm, and as a more immediate result, is a great method of delaying climax in a man (or woman).

Redirecting Sexual Energy to Delay Climax

This can be adapted for other uses.

As soon as the man feels the point of no return, he uses breathing techniques as previously described, and he or his lover sweeps the energy from his groin to wherever he wants it. For example, they may:

- Gently massage the testicles then stroke down his thighs and up his belly to his heart.
- Draw the energy from the penis up through his spine into his heart.

To charge energy from her into him, his lover can sweep the energy from his penis to his heart, then into her heart and out of her vagina back into his penis.

Following the Snake

During other tantric exercises, you may build up so much energy that it courses up your spine.

Go with it and you can experience higher states of being.

Related Chapters:

- Breathing

PEAKING

Peaking is an exercise that can be done during intercourse or masturbation. It is an effective way for men to last longer. It can also be used by either sex to build up sexual energy, which will increase sexual pleasure. It is done by starting and stopping stimulation at various stages of arousal.

First find your point of no return. Give the stages of your arousal a scale from zero to 10. Zero is no arousal and ten is orgasm. Nine is your point of no return—that is, the point where it wouldn't matter if you stopped stimulation; you would still climax. You want to get to a 7 or 8 and stay there until you choose to climax.

Once you reach level 8, stop stimulation and re-direct your focus. Once your arousal has gone down to a 5 or 6, restart stimulation. Do this a few times before allowing yourself to climax. Other patterns you can use are:

- Peak, plateau, peak higher, plateau etc.
- Peak, plateau, decrease, peak a little higher than before, decrease, peak a little higher still, etc.

You can also try any other patterns you can think of until you discover what will work to control your arousal level without having to stop completely. Make a goal to last 30 minutes without stopping.

If needed, you can use peaking during intercourse by taking your penis out and changing positions, massaging, switching to oral stimulation, etc., until your arousal goes down.

Tantric Peaking

For this to work, the man must be adept at controlling his climax.

As you make love, allow the sexual energy to grow naturally. After about 20 minutes, you may feel a decrease in sexual energy. Allow this to happen and just relax in this state together. Stay inside your lover, even if your penis becomes soft. After a while, your sexual energy will return and you can attain a higher feeling of ecstasy. Move however you wish. Allow this increase and decrease of sexual energy to happen as many times as you wish. When you're ready, allow yourselves to climax.

Related Chapters:

- Masturbation

TANTRIC MASSAGE

Basic Tantric Massage

Your lover lies on their front. Massage their whole back and when ready, concentrate on the lower back. Guide the energy from here up the spine. Next, massage the head, back of the legs and feet. Take your time.

Your lover turns over. If he is a man, massage his belly with sweeping clockwise movements around his navel. If she is a woman, massage her lower abdomen in the same manner. Rest your hands on your lover's solar plexus and synchronize your breathing.

When ready, sweep up over their chest and shoulders and down their arms and hands, then continue to massage their arms and hands.

When you're ready, come back to massaging the chest, then sweep up the middle of their chest (between the breasts if they're a woman) and towards their throat.

Rest your hand on their heart, with your other hand between the eyebrows. Next, massage their neck and throat. Rest one hand on their throat and the other on the back of the neck. When ready, massage their head, face, and scalp.

Move down and massage their groin. If your lover is a man, pay special attention to his perineum then continue to massage his penis and testicles. If she is a woman, massage her pubic mound and around her vagina.

Finish with whole-body sweeps: down the legs, then back up over the chest and down the arms.

Tantric Chakra Massage

Your lover lies naked.

Oil up your fingers and apply the oil in a slow clockwise motion to the first chakra for a few minutes.

Rest your hand there for a moment to feel the energy expanding before reapplying oil and moving on to the second chakra. Continue this process up through all the chakras.

When you get to the sixth chakra, use gentle upward sweeps from in between your lover's eyebrows to their hairline.

Do not apply oil for the seventh chakra, and return to a clockwise rubbing.

When ready, place one hand on the first chakra and one on the seventh. Imagine the energy between the chakras connecting through your lover's body.

Related Chapters:

- Chakras
- Breathing

TANTRIC DANCING

Seductively Solo

Find somewhere private, where you will not be disturbed. Put on some music you will enjoy dancing to in a sexy manner.

Begin to dance as if your lover is watching you. Slowly and sensually remove your clothing for your lover. Imagine them being in awe of your beauty.

Once you are completely naked, dance uninhibited. Feel the sexual energy rising through your chakras. Caress yourself as you move.

When you are ready, lie down and continue to caress yourself.

Touch every inch of your body, imagining you are being touched by your lover. Bring yourself to orgasm if you wish.

Releasing Stress through Dance

You can release any stress held in your body with by dancing to your choice of music. Let your body move as it wants. Shake and make noise so everything comes out.

The Dance of Two Snakes

Dance back-to-back with your lover, but do not lean back into them.

Imagine a snake sitting at the base of your spine and working its way up. Let your body move with the snake as it climbs up your back.

As it reaches your arms, allow them to rise so the snake can uncoil further up and out of your hands.

Feel the serpent collecting energy from the universe above and feeding back down your body through your chakras. The energy and the snake should weave around each other, vibrating in your body.

When you're ready, face your lover and join at your foreheads, merging your energies.

The Calming of the Tribal Urge

Put on some "animalistic" or "tribal-ish" music to dance to.

Dance with your lover, undressing as you do so, until you're both naked. Build up your sexual energy as you move. Focus your energy into your genitals while you gaze into each other's souls. Feel the desire for sex rising. When you're ready, give in to your desires, but do not climax.

Allow the intensity to diminish and just lay together, with your lover still inside you, or vice versa.

When your/his erection is no more, stand and face each other.

Play some easygoing music and dance for each other once again.

When you're ready, lay down and embrace each other. Breathe circularly, then just lay still together.

Body Shake

Put on some music to make you move and begin to shake only your right leg. Next, shake your left leg, then your hips, arms, hands, shoulders, and your head. Keep adding body parts until your whole body is moving to the beat.

Related Chapters:

- Chakras

TANTRIC ORAL

While giving mutual oral pleasure, you both imagine love energy flowing through your touch into your lover, thus building a circle of energy.

Whilst you are giving your partner exclusive oral pleasure, they vocalize whatever comes into the mind. It is uncensored and may or may not make sense.

Blindfold your lover and have them lie down. Taste their body all over and begin to give them oral pleasure. Indulge in your lover's taste. Allow the energy to flow between you. Do not bring your lover to climax. Instead, bring them close, then let the energy subside. Repeat the rising and subsiding of climax a number of times to build up energy.

When you are ready, place one hand on your lover's vagina or penis and the other on their heart or crown. Have your lover release the energy throughout their body.

Swap positions, and then bring each other to climax.

SEXUAL POSES FOR TANTRIC SEX

The best positions to use during tantric sex are those in which lovers feel most connected with your lover, and can look into each other's eyes and hold each other close.

Lotus

She crosses her ankles and draws her knees up. He kneels with his knees on either side of her and leans over her, resting on his hands. He can lean into her legs if she is flexible enough.

Clasping

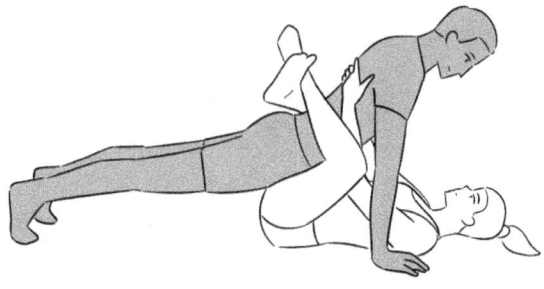

She lies on her back with her legs spread. He puts his groin to hers, keeping his body straight and supporting his weight on his toes and hands. She crosses her ankles around his waist. He presses his hips down, while pushing his upper body up off the floor at the same time.

Face to Face

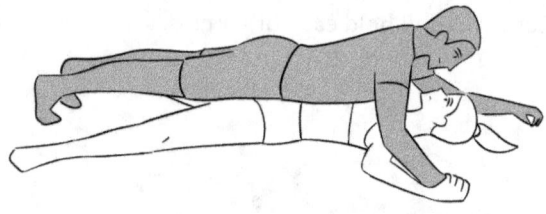

She lies flat on her back, legs spread. He lies on top of her, with his groin on hers. His legs are straight and his feet are together. He supports his weight on his toes. They grab each other's hands. He pushes down with his hips while lifting his upper body.

Yin and Yang

This is also known as Yab Yum. He sits cross-legged and she sits on top of him. They hold each other close, and she crosses her legs around his back.

AFTER CLIMAX

After either or both of you have climaxed, sit up in Yab Yum with your lover still inside you, or vice versa.

Take a deep breath in and picture drawing the energy of the ejaculation up the spine.

As you exhale, picture a golden mist coming down the spine.

30 MORE TANTRIC MEDITATIONS AND EXERCISES

Balancing Sexual Energy

Put your right index finger on the top of your nose between your eyes.

Exhale hard through your nose.

Close your right nostril with your thumb and breathe in to the count of seven. Release your right nostril and close your left nostril with your middle finger. Breathe out forcefully.

Continue to alternate the nostril you breathe in and out from. You can enhance the practice by contracting your PC muscle.

To stimulate your masculine energy, turn your head to the left and block your left nostril while you breathe. To stimulate your feminine energy, block your right nostril and turn your head to the right.

Bathing

While in the shower with your lover, soap up and turn your backs to each other. Rub against each other.

Cycling Love Energy

Place your right hand on your lover's heart while your lover does the same to you.

Visualize sending love energy from your heart down your arm and into your lover's heart.

Your left hand can be placed on any of yours or your lover's chakras in order to circulate the energy. Place it where ever you want the energy to go.

Divine Admiration

Slowly remove your lover's clothes.

As you expose each new part of their body, you both become aware of it.

When your lover is completely naked, they sit or lie down.

Caress each part of your lover's body, admiring it verbally as you go. For example, say, "These are the thighs of a magnificent being" or "These are beautiful buttocks," etc. When you've finished, transition to sex or just lie together.

Energy Focus

Sit back-to-back with your lover. Be close, but do not touch each other.

Close your eyes and focus on your spine. Shut off your attention to everything but the energy in between your two spines.

Energy Reading

Sit in the Yab Yum and synchronize your breathing.

When ready, close your eyes and let your hands explore your lover's body.

Whenever you feel like it, let your hands relax on a part of their body and say whatever comes into your mind, uncensored.

Food Play

Prepare a plate of bite-sized natural foods and include a glass of wine. Savor each bite and meditate on the flavors as if it is the first time you've tasted them. Being blindfolded will enhance the sense of taste.

Your lover is blindfolded and lies back comfortably while you feed them. Allow time for them to experience the smells, tastes, and textures of each piece, then pour a little wine into their mouth and allow them to experience it fully. Swap roles when you're ready.

Try these exercises in complete silence, and/or just enjoy a meal together outdoors without talking to each other.

Internal Listening

Put your thumbs in your ears and your fingers on the top of your head.

Listen to your breathing and any other internal sounds.

Laugh

Lie next to each other. Relax and stretch for a few minutes.

Laugh freely from your abdomens. Focus on your base chakras opening up. When your laughter naturally subsides, lie quietly and feel the sexual energy course through your bodies.

Lion Play

In a playful manner, both of you become lions.

Make sounds and move as lions would. When you are ready, approach each other.

Become territorial and ward each other off. Growl and circle warily. Become a little more aggressive and push on each other's paws, roaring loudly.

When you're ready and you naturally calm down, investigate each other. Smell and lick each other as wild beasts would. Become comfortable with each other. You may choose to mate, or just lie together as lions would. Afterward, come back to your human forms.

Moving Energy

Use your imagination and physical touch to move yours and/or your lover's energy around their body. You can move the energy to where ever you think it is needed.

While stimulating their genitals with one hand, imagine your breath going through your hand and into your lover's body. Use your other hand to move the energy to whichever chakra you want it to go to.

As you breathe back in, imagine the energy flowing back up from the chakra into your hand and cycling through your bodies. Keep breathing and visualizing the energy with your hands in these positions to create a cycle of energy. You can move the energy to other chakras if you wish.

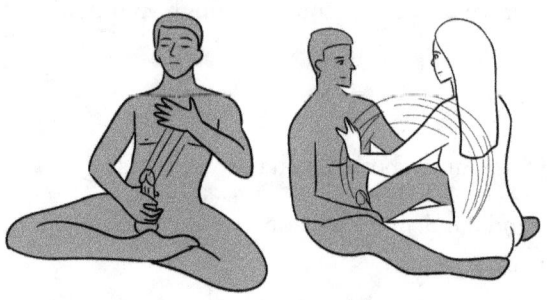

Music

Play your favorite music. Lie comfortable with your eyes closed and listen intently, letting the music fill your body. This can also be done with nature. That is, you can lie/sit outside and just listen to the sounds of nature.

Om

Sit opposite each other and synchronize your breathing.

When you're ready, chant "Ommmmm" together. Feel the vibration in your bodies and let it build naturally.

Opening of the Chakras

Exhale and thrust your pelvis forward, saying "Ooooo." Inhale and bend your back forward, saying, "Aaahhhhh." Repeat.

Do the same exercise using "ooooo" on the exhale and "ehhh-hhh" on the inhale, then using "oooo" and "uhhh."

Pelvic Thrusts

These can be done lying, squatting or standing. You can also change positions as you do them.

As you exhale, thrust your pelvis forward. On the inhale, thrust your pelvis backward. Swing your arms in time with your thrusts.

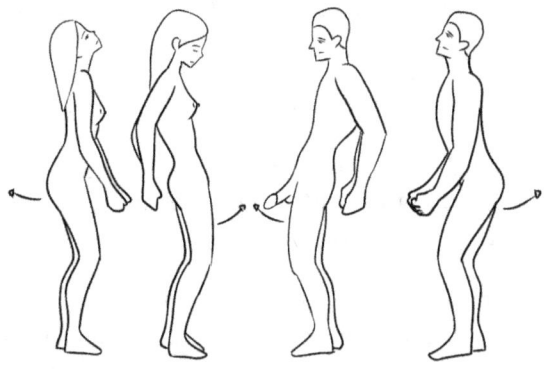

Praising Each Other

Sit together and think of three things you love or admire about your lover.

Take turns telling each other the three things, calling each other by name. For example, say "Mike, I really love the way you..."

Quenched Desires

Enter a meditative state.

You are the master and your lover is your servant. They will fulfill all your wishes.

Demand anything you want from them. Take as long as you need to fulfill all your desires. Next time, swap roles.

Returning to Earth

Stand opposite each other and visualize a spiral of energy from your heads to your groins.

Dance freely and make whatever sounds you want.

When you feel like it, calm down into cross-legged sitting positions, facing each other with your knees touching. Breathe in sync while swaying to loosen your bodies.

Breathe in and out of each of your chakras, starting from your base chakra. Move your way up your bodies until the energy is gathered at your crowns. Let this energy expand through your bodies and out into the universe. Lie down together for as long as you wish.

Sacrum Tap

Lay your lover on their stomach and tap on the area above their tailbone and below their waist. Next, run your thumbs up your lover's spine. Continue by tapping up on either side of your lover's spine with your fingertips. Finish with massage.

Seeing Your Lovers Soul

Sit opposite your lover and gaze into each other's eyes.

Begin full-stomach breathing and let all other concerns subside.

Do not speak. Look further into your lover's eyes. See their soul. Do this for as long as you wish.

Sensory Pleasure

Prepare a variety of pleasant scents and some fruits.

Blindfold your lover and get him/her to sit or lie down comfortably.

Introduce the different scents to your lover. They should smell each one deeply and separately. Next, take a piece of fruit and release its aroma by gently squeezing it.

Let your lover smell the fruit then place it on their lips so they know to allow you to place it in their mouth. Your lover should fully experience the taste and texture of the fruit, then allow the taste and smell to combine.

Swap roles.

Then, with both of you blindfolded, taste and smell each other in the same manner. Finish by making love, still blindfolded.

Sex Magic

Use visualization to manifest what you want from the universe.

Lie relaxed and visualize what you want.

Imagine sexual energy coursing through your body, enhancing the feeling you have when you have whatever it is you want.

When you are having sex or masturbating, recall this visualization and feeling, especially during high-pleasure states, including orgasm.

Sharing Desires

The two of you will share whatever desires come to your mind. They can be sexual or non-sexual.

Take turns saying "I want ..." and then say whatever comes to your mind.

Don't censor it. Everything is OK, including silence.

Sharing Loves Nature

Sit or kneel side by side with your lover. Get comfortable.

Each of you place a natural object of your choice, such as a flower or pebble, in front of you.

Take a couple of minutes to confide in your respective objects about your relationship.

Talk as if your lover was not there—that is, using the third person. Say anything you feel, positive or negative. This might be "I feel something is bothering her" or "I love the way he touches me when we make love," etc.

Continue to alternate who is talking every few minutes until the both of you feel you have finished sharing. Don't interrupt your lover when it is their turn.

Once you are finished, pick up your objects and imagine all the clutter in your minds flowing into them.

Place your object next to your lover, then place your head on the ground and ask for guidance from the universe. Drop all expectations and allow the wisdom to enter your mind, no matter what it is. If you wish, share the wisdom with your lover. Finish by taking your lover's object and returning it to nature, while they do the same for you.

Shiva Shakti Mudra

This is very effective for building energy.

Stand with your feet shoulder-width apart and with your knees slightly bent.

Take a few full-stomach breaths and get centered.

When you are ready, on the inhale sweep your arms up to collect the energy from the earth and bring it into your heart.

Exhale.

Inhale again, but this time, reach up to the sky and gather energy from the sky.

Sweep your arms down, crossing your hands over each other as you pass your face and pour the energy into your heart.

You can also send the energy out to others, like your lover or the world in general, by aiming your arms at them as opposed to into your heart.

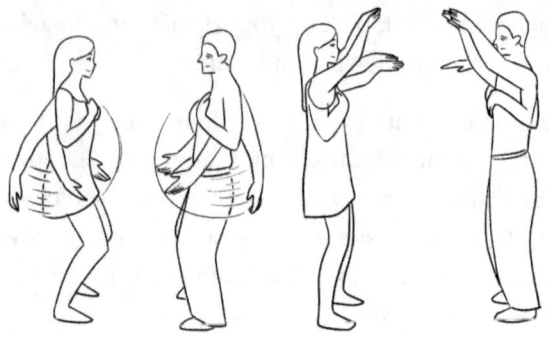

Singing

Blindfold your lover.

Hum a tune and whisper in their ear. Sing for your lover. Play an instrument if you wish.

Swap roles.

Smell

Take a shower together using only water or non-synthetic products so you do not overpower your natural scents.

Put on a blindfold and then smell all over your lover's body. Swap roles when you're ready. Finish with blindfolded sex.

Soulful Embrace

As you gaze into each other's eyes, slowly come together and embrace each other.

Synchronize your breath and become one.

When you're ready, separate slowly. Maintain eye contact as you separate.

Tantric Triangle

Visualize a triangle of white light in between your eyes, pointing down toward the back of your tongue.

Taste

Lightly touch around your lover's mouth and lips. Begin to touch the rest of their face.

Blindfold your lover and feed them various bite-sized foods of different tastes and textures.

Related Chapters:

- Chakras
- Breathing

THANKS FOR READING

Dear reader,

Thank you for reading *Learn Tantric Sex*.

If you enjoyed this book, please leave a review where you bought it. It helps more than most people think.

Don't forget your FREE book chapters!

You will also be among the first to know of FREE review copies, discount offers, bonus content, and more.

Go to:

https://offers.SFNonfictionBooks.com/Free-Chapters

Thanks again for your support.

REFERENCES

Richardson, D. (2003). *The Heart of Tantric Sex: A Unique Guide to Love and Sexual Fulfillment.* Bedroom Books.

Richardson, D. Richardson, M. (2010). *Tantric Sex for Men: Making Love a Meditation.* Destiny Books.

Riley, D. Riley, K. (2002). *Tantric Secrets for Men: What Every Woman Will Want Her Man to Know about Enhancing Sexual Ecstasy.* Destiny Books.

AUTHOR RECOMMENDATIONS

Discover all the Secrets for Improving Your Sex Life

You'll love this book because it is the last sex-manual you'll ever need!

Get it now.

www.SFNonfictionBooks.com/Great-Sex

Discover How to Use Yoga as Medicine

Add this book to your collection, because with it you can use yoga to heal your mind, body, and spirit.

Get it now.

www.SFNonfictionBooks.com/Curing-Yoga

ABOUT AVENTURAS

Aventuras has three passions: travel, writing, and self-improvement. She is also blessed (or cursed) with an insatiable thirst for general knowledge.

Combining these things, Miss Viaje spends her time exploring the world and learning. She takes what she discovers and shares it through her books.

www.SFNonfictionBooks.com

amazon.com/author/aventuras
goodreads.com/AventurasDeViaje
facebook.com/AuthorAventuras
instagram.com/AuthorAventuras

www.ingramcontent.com/pod-product-compliance
Lightning Source LLC
Chambersburg PA
CBHW071035080526
44587CB00015B/2620